Bill Clinton

Published by Raintree Steck-Vaughn Publishers, an imprint of Steck-Vaughn Company.

Planned and produced by The Creative Publishing Company
Editors: Christine Lawrie and Pam Wells

Library of Congress Cataloging-in-Publication Data

Holland, Gini.
    Bill Clinton / Gini Holland; illustrated by Gary Rees.
      p.   cm. — (First biographies)
    Summary: Introduces the life and accomplishments of the Democrat who was elected president to two successive terms, 1992 and 1996.
    ISBN 0-8172-4450-6
    1. Clinton, Bill, 1946- — Juvenile literature.   2. Presidents — United States — Biography — Juvenile literature. [1. Clinton, Bill, 1946-   .
2. Presidents.]   I. Rees, Gary, ill.   II. Title.   III. Series.
E886.H65   1997
973.929'092 — dc21
[B]   96-39485
                                                 CIP
                                                 AC

Printed and bound in the United States
1 2 3 4 5 6 7 8 9 0 W 01 00 99 98 97

FIRST BIOGRAPHIES

Bill Clinton

Gini Holland
Illustrated by Gary Rees

RSVP
RAINTREE
Steck-Vaughn
PUBLISHERS
The Steck-Vaughn Company

Austin, Texas

Bill Clinton came a long way to become President of the United States. He was born in Hope, Arkansas, on August 19, 1946. Arkansas is one of the poorest states in the country, and Bill's family did not have much money. Two months before Bill was born, his father was killed in a car accident. His mother, Virginia, named her baby William Jefferson Blythe IV, after his father.

They lived with Virginia's parents. Bill called his grandparents "Mawmaw" and "Pawpaw." They taught him to read and say numbers while he was still in his high chair.

Hope is circled by pine trees and farms. Townsfolk call it the "Watermelon Capital of the World." Trains pass right through Hope on the way to nearby Texas or Louisiana. From the porch of his grandparents' house, Bill could hear the train whistle as it left town.

In 1949, his mother left for New Orleans to learn to be a nurse. President Clinton remembers visiting her with Mawmaw and then saying goodbye. He remembers his mother on her knees, crying, at the train station. When he talks about how hard it is for single parents to work and care for their children, he thinks of that day.

Finally, his mother came home with her nursing degree. Then, in 1950, she married Roger Clinton. They moved to their own house. His new "Daddy" bought him a toy train. He also had a cowboy outfit so he could pretend to be his childhood hero, Hopalong Cassidy.

In 1953, they moved to Hot Springs, Arkansas. The next year, the Supreme Court said African-American children had the right to go to the same schools as white children.

Rights like these are called civil rights. They are about being fair to everyone. But Bill had already learned from Pawpaw how to treat people fairly. Back then, most stores in the South sold their goods only to whites or only to blacks. But Pawpaw let everybody in his grocery store. Bill later said "Before I was big enough to see over the counter, I learned from him to look up to people other folks looked down upon."

Bill started high school in 1960. In the same year, his new hero, John Kennedy, was elected President. All over the country, people began to march and work for civil rights. Bill talked it over with his mother. His mother was not surprised at how much he knew. "He started reading the newspaper in first grade," she explained.

She told Bill to study hard, and he did. He was also junior class president and was in many school clubs and plays. Bill was the best saxophone player in his school band. In his spare time, he and two friends started a jazz band called The Kingsmen.

While Bill was in school, big things were taking place in the world. The United States started helping the government of South Vietnam. Over the years this turned into helping the South Vietnamese fight a war. It was a war in which Bill might have to fight once he was old enough for the army.

Then Bill was able to go to Boys State, where young people learn about government. He was elected Boys State Senator for Arkansas and went to Boys Nation in Washington, D.C.

In Washington, he had lunch with Arkansas Senator J. William Fulbright. Bill liked his ideas. Fulbright did not think American soldiers should be fighting in Vietnam.

The best part of the 1963 trip happened in the White House Rose Garden. Bill shook hands with President Kennedy! Overjoyed, he brought the photograph of this meeting home to his mother.

Four months later, President Kennedy was shot and killed. Bill Clinton lost his hero.

Clinton started at Georgetown University, in Washington, D.C., in 1964. It was a year of change for the United States, too. The Civil Rights Bill became law, and Congress sent more soldiers to fight in Vietnam. Many people thought this war was wrong. Clinton took part in both the civil rights and peace movements.

In 1968, Dr. Martin Luther King, Jr., was killed. Bill Clinton remembers where he was. He stood on his college dormitory roof and saw the black neighborhoods burning. People were rioting. He put a red cross on his white car. Then he and a friend drove food and blankets to a church in a burned-out neighborhood.

Clinton graduated and won a Rhodes scholarship to Oxford University in England. "Mother," he joked, "how do you think I'll look in English tweed?"

At Oxford in 1969, he got a letter from the United States military. They wanted him to fight in the Vietnam War. Clinton had helped set up marches against this war. However, he did not think all war was wrong. He decided to go home and join the military reserves. This way, he could serve without fighting in the war he hated.

But then, President Nixon started a lottery. If you got a high number, you would not be drafted. Bill got a high number. So he was able to go back to Oxford and stayed on at graduate school with his friends. Later, when he became President, he made one of these friends, Robert Reich, his secretary of labor. Another, Strobe Talbot, became his deputy secretary of state.

17

After leaving Oxford, he got a scholarship to Yale Law School where he met his future wife, Hillary Rodham. They both studied hard, but they also worked hard for peace.

In 1973, they got their law degrees. Hillary found a job in Washington, D.C. Bill went home and started teaching law at the University of Arkansas. A year later, he ran for Congress and lost, but this helped voters get to know him.

Bill and Hillary were married in 1975, in the little lake house he had bought for her as a surprise. The next year, Bill's political career began to grow. He became the state attorney general of Arkansas. Then, in 1979, when Bill was only 33 years old, he became governor of Arkansas.

Just a year later, his daughter Chelsea was born. It meant a lot to him to be able to hold his baby in his arms. He thought, "My father never got to do this."

Clinton lost the next election for governor. Some voters were angry with him because he had raised taxes to pay for better schools. At the time, Arkansas schools were the worst in the country. Soon voters realized he had been right, and in January 1983, he was elected again. He held the office of governor for the next ten years.

There had not been a Democratic President for the last three elections. In 1991, Clinton decided it was time to try and change this. At first, he had a tough time getting the Democratic Party to choose him to run for President. But Clinton kept trying.

People liked what he had to say. When he was finally chosen, he started calling himself "The Comeback Kid." The Republicans' choice, George Bush, was already President. He wanted to get elected again.

Clinton chose Senator Al Gore as his running mate for Vice President. Gore knew more about the environment than most people in the government. George Bush seemed to care more about business than the environment. Then Bush broke a promise and raised taxes. Many voters did not like that.

Bill Clinton showed he knew about peoples' problems. He knew that money, or the economy, was the big problem for most voters. The newspapers said that Bush did not even know how to shop in a grocery store! Unlike Bush, Clinton knew how much a loaf of bread cost. Bush fought back. He said Clinton had run away from the Vietnam War.

It was a close race, but on November 3, 1992, Clinton and Gore won the election. In his speech that night, Clinton told America, "With high hopes and brave hearts...the American people have voted to make a new beginning."

President Clinton's wife, Hillary, played a big part in his victory. She gave him advice and even finished a speech when his voice gave out. Strongly loved by many, she was also strongly disliked by others. She is very smart and speaks her own mind. Some people do not like the First Lady to be that strong.

President Clinton gave her the job of trying to make health care better. But it was hard to get things changed, and it did not work. Many people blamed Hillary.

Republicans started looking good to voters again. A great many Republicans were elected to Congress. There were more Republicans than Democrats. This made it very difficult for President Clinton to run the country. The Republicans tried to push their own ideas into law. But many of their ideas frightened voters. Clinton would not let them become law. This made many voters like him more. They blamed Republicans for not getting anything done.

Clinton made popular and important decisions about Bosnia and the Middle East. He got the Israeli Prime Minister, Yitzhak Rabin, to shake hands with the Palestinian Liberation Organization leader, Yasir Arafat. They made a peace agreement.

The economy was good for both business and workers. Business did well, partly because Clinton pushed through NAFTA, the North American Free Trade Agreement. NAFTA made it easier for the United States to do business with its neighbors, Mexico and Canada. At home, nine million more jobs opened up. All this made Clinton well-liked by many voters.

Bob Dole had been a powerful leader of the United States Senate. Now he wanted the Republican party back in the White House. He thought Clinton was bad for business and bad for the country. He decided to run against him in the 1996 election. At 73, Dole was much older than Clinton. Bob Dole had been badly wounded in World War II. Also he had a long career in the Senate.

As part of the election campaign, the two men appeared together on television. They were asked questions about what they would do if they were elected. Each one tried to persuade the people watching to vote for him.

In their first debate, both men did well. President Clinton said "We're better off than we were four years ago. Let's keep it going." He asked Americans to help him build a "...bridge to the 21st century."

In the next debate, when Dole said bad things about President Clinton, many voters did not like it. Later, the President said, "When they call names, you've got to look at the facts.... You don't need to call anybody any names."

On November 5, 1996, President Clinton became the first Democratic President to be elected again in over 50 years. He was inaugurated on January 20, 1997.

President Clinton planned to keep working to make America safe and strong. He wanted to keep the economy growing. Keeping the environment, the air and water, clean was very important to him. He said he planned to do this "...so our children will be growing up next to parks, not poison...." And he still had plans to improve health care for everyone.

He had a big job ahead of him, but he also had many Americans who wanted to help him reach his goals. With their help, he would take the United States into the 21st century.

Key Dates

1946 Born in Hope, Arkansas, on August 19. His mother names him William Jefferson Blythe IV.

1963 Goes to Washington, D.C., as a Senator for Boys Nation and meets President Kennedy at the White House.

1968 Graduates from Georgetown University and wins a Rhodes Scholarship to study at Oxford University in England.

1973 Graduates from Yale University Law School.

1975 Marries Hillary Rodham.

1979 Begins first two-year term as governor of Arkansas.

1980 Daughter Chelsea is born on February 27.

1993 Sworn in as the forty-second President of the United States on January 20.

Brings together Israeli Prime Minister Yitzhak Rabin and Palestinian Liberation Organization leader Yasir Arafat to make a peace agreement on September 13.

1996 Elected President again on November 5.

1997 Sworn in for second term as President of the United States on January 20.